Transform Daily

Kelly Wenner

www.soulstrengthfit.com

CONTENTS

Welcome to Transform Daily

Welcome to a 56-day journey designed to strengthen your faith and help you become more like Christ. Each day, you will dive into scripture, reflect on God's word, and take practical steps to live out your faith.

During the next 56 days, you will receive six daily devotionals per week to guide your time in the Word. (Sundays are intended to be a time of fellowship with a community of believers.)

How to Use This Devotional

Each day's devotional includes:

1. A Bible Verse(s)
Start with the day's scripture.

2. Reflection
Consider the day's message and how it applies to your life.

3. Action Steps
Practical ways to live out your faith.

You are encouraged to journal your thoughts and prayers as you go through each day. This is your personal journey with God, and these pages are here to support and guide you.

Connect and Share:

You are invited to pair these devotionals with the full faith-based fitness program: SoulStrength Fit Transform Daily 8 Week Challenge. Here you will find strength training workouts that accompany the devotionals, Christ-centered nutrition and health coaching, and an audio version of the devotionals as well.
Visit www.soulstrengthfit.com for more information.

Week 1 Devotionals

Transform Daily

Day 1: A Living Sacrifice

Today's Bible Verse

Read: Romans 12:1-2

Reflection

To fully offer yourself up as a servant to God, you must first trust in His kindness and goodness. Reflect on how your ability to serve God by obeying Him and serving others is directly related to the level of trust and confidence you have in His kindness and goodness.

Spend a few moments reflecting on the ways God has demonstrated kindness, goodness, and grace in your life. List as many examples as you can. Has He answered prayers, shown forgiveness, given blessings?

We are told to "offer our bodies as living sacrifices." This includes our arms, hands, legs, and all they are capable of doing. It encompasses all parts of who we are: our thoughts, energy, time, and abilities. How might this manifest in your life?

Take Action

How can you use your body to serve God this week? Are there people God has placed in your life whom He may want you to serve as you offer your body as a living sacrifice to Him? Decide who you can serve this week. Decide how best to use your time and energy to be open and ready to be used by God.

When moments come this week where you feel anything but a holy and pleasing living sacrifice for God, pause where you are. Ask Him to renew your mind and refresh your strength, giving you the ability to love Him by loving and serving others.
With the intention of seeking ways to give yourself to God and seek His good, pleasing, and perfect will in all you do, read Romans 12:1-2 once again.

3

Day 2: Forgiveness

Today's Bible Verse

Read: Matthew 6:5-15

Reflection

Forgiveness is so important to Jesus that He ties the forgiveness we give others to being forgiven ourselves. There is a profound connection between receiving forgiveness and offering it to others. We often hope that God will be more forgiving of us than we sometimes are of others. Would you say that you are as forgiving as you could be? Do you hold others to higher standards than you hold yourself?

True forgiveness can be a long journey, involving a quest for justice, managing feelings of anger or hurt, or simply acknowledging the wrong that needs to be forgiven. Perhaps there is a lingering grudge or persistent feeling in your heart, even after some time has passed. Who do you need to forgive? What is the next step you need to take on your path to forgiveness?

Read Matthew 6:5-15 once more. Listen for the simplicity of Jesus' example of prayer. Which line of the prayer speaks to you most today?

Take Action

- Identify someone you need to forgive and take the first step toward forgiveness.
- Reflect on areas where you expect more from others than from yourself.
- Pray for the ability to forgive and to be forgiven, using Jesus' example in Matthew 6:5-15.

Day 3: Follow Jesus

Today's Bible Verse

Read: John 12:23-26

Reflection

What does this verse mean? "He who loves his life will lose it, while the man who hates his life in this world will keep it."

The person who "loves his life" is someone who is living for the now, as if this present life is all there is. He is living in a way that contradicts Jesus' command, "Don't lay up treasure on earth." His focus is on storing up treasures on Earth rather than on serving Jesus.

The person who "hates his life" is storing up treasures in heaven and living in a way that honors and obeys God. His primary focus is following and serving Jesus. He will forfeit pleasures or temptations that stand in the way of obeying and serving God.

Sometimes storing up treasure for this life might show itself simply by becoming caught up in all of life's distractions and the constant busyness of day-to-day living. Or it might be striving for personal success, status, or comfort. In what ways do life's distractions prevent you from thriving and growing as a Christian? What might you do differently to keep your mind set on storing up treasure in heaven?

We read in Matthew 16:23-24: Then Jesus said to his disciples, "Whoever wants to be my disciple must deny themselves and take up their cross and follow me. For whoever wants to save their life will lose it, but whoever loses their life for me will find it."

Saving life is not referring to salvation from hell. It's referring to having fullness of life, in this life and in the life to come. And losing life refers to bypassing sinful tendencies or temptations to choose the better life God has in store when you follow Him.

A big part of taking up your cross daily is denying sinful thoughts that come up during the day. To "take up your cross" is something that has to take place in your thoughts. When thoughts that aren't pleasing to God come to your mind during the day, you "put them to death" on an inner "cross." A judging thought toward your friend pops up, for example, or perhaps a grumbling thought of dissatisfaction as you think about all you have to do today. Maybe you have a tendency to be judgmental toward your in-laws, critical of your spouse, envious of others, harsh toward neighbors, or angry at your kids. As these thoughts come up in your mind, you choose to deny them.

As you say "no" to the temptation of allowing these negative thoughts to persist, over time you will notice that those thoughts don't come as often anymore. It becomes easier for you to be kind, warm, and patient with the people around you. This is what true discipleship is all about. It's living a life that follows after Jesus. What did Jesus do in His daily life? His answer to temptation was: "Not My will, but Yours, be done." (Luke 22:42). He took up His cross and denied Himself. His temptations never resulted in sin – in word, in thought, or in deed.

What thoughts regularly pop up for you that don't honor God? What thoughts might you feel convicted to change? In which areas of your life might God be asking you to take up your cross?

Take Action

- In what ways are you most distracted by the demands, pleasures, and goals of this world? In what ways do you live and act as if this life is all there is? What could you do differently - whether in action or mindset - to live to the fullest now while simultaneously serving and obeying God and storing up treasure in the life to come?
- Think of 2 or 3 situations in which you can put selfish desires behind your desire to serve God. This week, even when I want to _____, I will _____.
- In your thoughts and words, what two areas can you begin to grow more Christ-like in your dedication to daily taking up your cross? I am not taking up my cross when I allow myself to think _____ and _____.

Read John 12:23-26. What might God be saying to you in these verses today?

Day 4: Trials and Difficulties

Today's Bible Verse

Read: James 1:2-12

Reflection

It's rare that we consider our trials to be "pure joy." Reflect on the past week: How did you respond to the trials, problems, or difficult situations you encountered? In what ways do you feel you need more strength or greater perseverance?

Think about a specific trial, whether past or present. How has your faith in God helped you handle this situation? Did it impact the situation itself, the way you dealt with it, or how you felt you should respond?

The perseverance gained through trials is invaluable for becoming "mature and complete, not lacking anything." Consider how you might grow more mature and complete through any current trials or difficulties you're facing. What might God be wanting to cultivate in you? Ask God for the wisdom needed to grow through these challenging situations.

Take Action

- Reflect on a recent trial or difficulty you have faced and how you responded to it. Pray for the strength and perseverance to face future challenges with faith and trust in God.
- Think about a particular trial you are currently facing. How has your faith in God helped you deal with this situation? Reflect on how you can more deeply rely on your faith to navigate the situation.
- Consider ways you can grow more mature and complete through your current trials. What might God be wanting to cultivate in you? Ask God for the wisdom needed to grow through this difficult situation.

Read James 1:2-12 once more, noticing words or phrases that stick with you the most. Meditate on these words and how they can guide you through your trials.

7

Day 5: Rooted in Christ

Today's Bible Verse

Read: Ephesians 4:21-24

Reflection

We are told to set our minds on things above, not on earthly things. This is because our actions stem from our thoughts. Take a moment to reflect—can you trace your sinful actions back to thoughts that are out of alignment with the Spirit? Think of specific examples where your mindset has led you to live in a way that doesn't honor God. It might be an unkind or unloving attitude toward others, judgmental or harsh words spoken, or feelings of envy fueled by thoughts of dissatisfaction. Consider how your thoughts can negatively impact your actions.

Knowing that actions stem from our thoughts, two important questions to ask ourselves when considering how in tune we are with the Holy Spirit are:
- How discouraged am I lately?
- How irritated am I lately?

How would you answer these questions? To flourish as a Christian, the love and peace of God must be growing in us. When it is, we are less easily discouraged and less easily irritated. Remember: we can't make ourselves loving or joyful. A tree's job is not to try to bear fruit; the tree's job is to abide near the river. How are you doing lately with abiding near the river?

Take Action

- In the week ahead, when you feel your mind begin to take a downward spiral, purposefully and mindfully shift your thoughts. Begin to reflect, ponder, and think about things that are admirable and lovely. Maybe this for you is a sunset, a friend's smile, your child's laugh, a good novel, or music that makes you feel alive. Consider some of the good things God has put in your life and allow your mind to dwell on them.
- Begin your day this way as you enjoy your morning coffee, and each time you are in the car, draw blessings to mind. Maybe set a timer to go off every hour as a reminder to set your mind on good and lovely things. Make this a focused practice for the week.

"Blessed are those... who delight in the law of the Lord and meditate on his law day and night. They are like a tree planted by streams of water, which yields its fruit in season and whose leaves do not wither - whatever they do prospers."

Throughout your day, pray continuously for the ability to remain rooted in Christ, planted by the streams of His living water, capable of producing fruit that glorifies Him and blesses those around you.

Read Ephesians 4:21-24 once again, considering how the attitude of your mind may need to be made new.

Day 6: Use Your Gifts

Today's Bible Verse

Read: Matthew 25:14-21

Reflection

What was the criteria used in distributing the money? (v15)

Quote:

"The Tragedy of the Unopened Gift" by Gregg Levoy:
Sinful patterns of behavior that never get confronted and changed,
Abilities and gifts that never get cultivated and deployed -
Until weeks become months
And months turn into years,
And one day you're looking back on a life of deep, intimate, gut-wrenchingly honest conversations you never had;
Great bold prayers never prayed,
Exhilarating risks you never took,
Sacrificial gifts you never offered,
Lives you never touched,
And you're sitting in a recliner with a shriveled soul,
And forgotten dreams, and you realize there was a world of desperate need,
And a great God calling you to be part of something bigger than yourself -
You see the person you could have become but did not;
You never followed your calling.
You never got out of the boat.

What might God be calling you to do? What gifts are you burying?
How might God be wanting to use you and stretch you and grow you?
Read Matthew 25:14-21 once more, and imagine the many ways you can be a good steward of whatever gifts He has given you - large or small.

Take Action

- Identify one fruit of the Spirit that you want to focus on this week. Pray for God's help in developing this quality in your life.
- Reflect on practical ways you can demonstrate this quality in your interactions with others.
- At the end of each day, take a moment to reflect on how you demonstrated the fruit of the Spirit and where you can improve.

Read Galatians 5:22-23 again and ask God to fill you with His Spirit, helping you to live out these qualities in your daily life.

Week 2
Devotionals

Transform Daily

Day 1: Are You Available for God?

Today's Bible Verse

Read: Exodus 3:1-15

Reflection

"Here I am." This statement is one of availability, not location. Moses made himself available to God, pausing in his journey to take in the sight that God had set before him.

In your busy and hurried life, how often do you find the time to stop and say, "Here I am, Lord"? How often do you pause and genuinely tell the Lord, "Here I am, ready to do Your will. Use me for Your glory. Use me to bless those around me, even if it means stepping out of my comfort zone or doing things I might not particularly want to do"?

It is in these moments that real change occurs in our character, attitudes, walk with God, and overall life.

Can you be open this week to taking the time to become aware of God's presence and offer the statement, "Here I am, Lord," ready for whatever He might be calling you to do?

When Moses asked, "Who am I that I should go to Pharaoh and bring the Israelites out of Egypt?" God reassured him with the promise of His own presence.
When you don't feel good enough, strong enough, capable, wise, or special enough to face the challenges before you, remember that God is with you. Stand firm on these five promises:

- God is with me: "Do not fear, for I am with you."
- God is my God: "Do not look anxiously about you, for I am your God."
- God will strengthen me: "I will strengthen you."
- God will help me: "Surely I will help you."
- God will uphold me: "Surely I will uphold you with My righteous right hand."

Take Action

- Reflect on your availability to God. Are you taking time to pause and be aware of His presence in your life? This week, make a conscious effort to say, "Here I am, Lord," and be open to His calling.
- When you feel inadequate or overwhelmed, remind yourself of God's promises. Write them down and place them somewhere visible to reinforce these truths in your heart and mind.
- Take a moment each day to pray for the strength, help, and support that God promises. Trust in His presence and His ability to uphold you.

Read Exodus 3:1-15 once more, focusing on Moses' responses and God's reassurances. Meditate on how you can apply these lessons in your own life.

Day 2: Do You Take Time to Thank God?

Today's Bible Verse

Read: Luke 17:11-19

Reflection

It can be easy to read this passage and assume we would act differently in the place of the lepers who didn't come back to thank Jesus. We wouldn't have been so ungrateful. We would have recognized the power of God in the healing. Or would we? Would we be so excited by our change in circumstance that we would forget to thank God? Put yourself into the story as one of the lepers. What happens?

It can be easy to forget to thank God for the good things in our lives, yet easy to complain when things go wrong. Consider this past week. What has been good? Have you thanked God for these good things? Would you like to do so now?

Take Action

- Reflect on the past week and identify the good things that have happened. Take a moment to thank God for these blessings.
- Make a habit of regularly thanking God for His goodness, even in the midst of difficulties. Consider setting aside a specific time each day to express gratitude.
- Put yourself into the story of the lepers. Imagine you are one of them. How does it feel to be healed? How important is it to return and thank Jesus?

Read Luke 17:11-19 once again. When you finish reading, take a few moments in prayer, and bring to Jesus an area of your life, or situation you are facing, that is in need of healing. Or perhaps there is someone on your mind that you'd like to place in the Lord's healing presence. Jesus is there, listening to your request.

Day 3: How Do You Handle Your Weaknesses?

Today's Bible Verse

Read: 2 Corinthians 12:6-10

Reflection

In today's reading, Paul mentions that he was given a thorn. He recognized God, not Satan, as the source of this thorn, understanding that its purpose was to keep him humble and reliant on Christ's power. Anything that God gives us to keep us humble and prayerfully dependent on Him is a great gift—even when that gift brings us pain.

What thorns—whether physical, emotional, or situational—are weaknesses for you? Perhaps something you struggle with daily or have repeatedly asked God to remove.

In what ways have you felt strengthened by God through your weaknesses and difficulties? Have they led you to rely on Him more, to seek Him more earnestly?

Looking ahead, how might your current struggles or thorns be used to remain humble, prayerful, and dependent on God's strength?

The Bible never specifies what Paul's "thorn in the flesh" was, likely for a good reason. Each of us has our own thorn, whether mental, emotional, or physical. If Paul had identified his thorn specifically, Christians might struggle to relate if their own afflictions were different. The vagueness allows us all to identify with Paul to some degree in our sufferings. But the specific nature of Paul's thorn isn't the point. The point is the purpose behind it: God gave it to Paul to keep him humble and constantly in need of His grace.

Often our struggles, or "thorns," can leave us feeling inadequate, weak, unimportant, or insignificant. Consider what negative behaviors you are prone to when you come face to face with your weaknesses or your feelings of inadequacy.

Do you:

- withdraw from others
- want to quit
- want to rely on your own strength and ability
- project false confidence
- get angry, frustrated, or defensive
- become overwhelmed by anxiety

Take Action

- Talk to God honestly now about how you feel you handle your weaknesses. Perhaps ask for a greater sense of his grace and strength during your times of struggle or feelings of inadequacy. Notice in the week ahead when these feelings emerge, or when your negative behaviors in response to these feelings begin. When they do, pause, and humbly ask God for his strength and grace to see you through.
- Be encouraged: trials not only make us rely on God, but they are also refining us just as gold is refined by fire.

Scripture Encouragement:

- 2 Corinthians 4:8-10 - "We are afflicted in every way, but not crushed; perplexed, but not driven to despair; persecuted, but not forsaken; struck down, but not destroyed; always carrying in the body the death of Jesus, so that the life of Jesus may also be manifested in our bodies."
- 1 Peter 4:12-13 - "Beloved, do not be surprised at the fiery trial when it comes upon you to test you, as though something strange were happening to you. But rejoice insofar as you share Christ's sufferings, that you may also rejoice and be glad when his glory is revealed."
- Hebrews 12:11 - "For the moment all discipline seems painful rather than pleasant, but later it yields the peaceful fruit of righteousness to those who have been trained by it."
- 2 Corinthians 4:17 - "For this light momentary affliction is preparing for us an eternal weight of glory beyond all comparison."
- Read 2 Corinthians 12:6-10 once again, considering all the ways your weaknesses can make you stronger in the Lord.

Day 4 – Need to Be Healed

Today's Bible Verse

Read: Mark 5:25-34

Reflection

Let the scene of this Gospel passage really sink in. Imagine the sights, the smells, and the sounds. Imagine the woman with the hemorrhage and all she has endured at the hands of all those physicians. Imagine what it's like for her to live so poor, and the rejection she must feel in her community.

Picture her in the crowd and imagine what she's feeling.

Who is Jesus to her?
Who is He to you?

"Who touched me," Jesus asked. Why do you think He asked that? Consider how she felt at that moment. He desires to meet the one who has demonstrated such faith in Him. He desires to meet and know you.

Take Action

- Read Mark 5:25-34 once more. Really imagine the scene with all of your senses.
- After reading, reflect on an area in your life where you'd like to ask Jesus for healing.
- Take a moment to pray, asking Jesus to meet you in this place and to bring His healing touch.

Day 5 – Proverbs 31 Woman of Noble Character

Today's Bible Verse

Read: Proverbs 31:10-31

Reflection

As you reflect on this beautiful piece of scripture, remember that it's not describing one specific woman. Rather, it offers a portrait of the kind of woman a king should seek in a wife—a virtuous woman who fears the Lord. This passage depicts a woman of experience, the type of woman a young wife would grow into, not necessarily the one he would marry immediately. Proverbs 31 outlines the virtues of a godly woman, the characteristics that God desires to cultivate in the heart and life of every woman who follows Him. As you revisit the passage, take note of the character traits described in this noble woman. Whether you are married or single, have children or not, are young or older, consider which of these traits you can nurture in your own life.

A Proverbs 31 woman is defined by her virtue and character. The emphasis is not only on what she does, but on who she becomes. Becoming this woman of virtuous character is made possible through God's grace and is developed through a deep connection with Him; it is not achieved by striving or works alone. Reflect on the following virtues demonstrated by the woman described in this passage:

- She is trustworthy.
- She is a blessing to her husband (or a blessing to others).
- She is an eager worker.
- She is resourceful.
- She is industrious.
- She is well-prepared.
- She is strong and dignified.
- She is wise.

These virtues are those that a woman who loves God will naturally develop as she grows and matures in her walk with the Lord. As you consider this list, don't feel overwhelmed; remember that becoming a Proverbs 31 woman is a journey. Which of these virtues do you feel most called to cultivate at this stage in your life and in your walk with God?

Take Action

- Reread this passage once more, and consider the following questions:

    ◦ What does this chapter tell me about God?
    ◦ What is the context and purpose of this chapter?
    ◦ What does this chapter tell me about my relationship with God?
    ◦ What does this chapter tell me about my own heart?
    ◦ How can I take what I've learned here and apply it to my life?

Day 6 – Abundance and Blessing

Today's Bible Verse

Read: John 21:1-14

Reflection

This is the third time the disciples encounter Jesus after His resurrection. In this meeting, Jesus guides the disciples, transforming a fruitless night of fishing into a moment of success and joy. Even before they recognize Him, Jesus is already at work, bringing abundance and blessing into a tired and seemingly hopeless situation.

Imagine you are one of the disciples alongside Simon Peter in this story. How do you feel after working all night and catching nothing? What is your mental state? How do you feel physically?

Now, think of a time in your own life when you experienced similar feelings. Have you ever faced a situation that felt helpless and overwhelming? Maybe you felt mentally and physically exhausted, as if you were working tirelessly with nothing to show for it, with no end in sight, and no apparent way for the situation to improve.

Now, picture yourself as one of the disciples in the boat. How do you respond when the man on the shore tells you to cast your net on the right side of the boat? Are you annoyed? Frustrated? Simply exhausted? Or perhaps you feel a glimmer of curiosity. Can you relate this emotion to a personal experience with the Lord? Maybe there was a time when you didn't understand what He was doing, where He was, or how anything good could come from your situation. How did you respond to Jesus then?

When Simon Peter realizes that the man on the shore is Jesus, how do you respond in your heart when John says, "It is the Lord"? What do you do next? How do you envision your first encounter with the Lord? What actions do you take as you imagine what that moment would be like?

Take Action

- Read John 21:1-14 once again. Notice how the disciples catch a huge number of fish when they listen to Jesus telling them to change their way of working.
- Reflect on an area in your life where you might feel stuck or exhausted. Consider honestly—might Jesus be challenging you to change something in your life?
- Take a moment to pray, asking for the wisdom and guidance to recognize Jesus' presence and direction in your current situation.

Week 3
Devotionals

Transform Daily

Day 1 – Peacemakers Do Not Envy

Today's Bible Verse

Read: James 3:13-18

Reflection

Envy can be defined as resenting God's goodness to others while overlooking His goodness in your own life. It involves focusing on others' blessings instead of your own. It's desire mixed with resentment. We often believe that if we had someone else's success, opportunities, beauty, or fortune, we would finally be happy. Reflect honestly: with which people or in which situations do you struggle most with envy?

Are there steps you can take to reduce these feelings or avoid triggering them? For instance, if you find yourself struggling with envy after spending time on social media, would cutting back on your Facebook or Instagram usage help you avoid falling into the envy trap? Or could you intentionally start practicing gratitude, counting your own blessings instead of constantly tallying those of others?

Envy often stems from comparison. Comparing what you have to what others possess is a sure way to make yourself miserable. This fixation on comparison inevitably leads to noticing someone who seems to have more, leaving you feeling inadequate. The truth is, there will always be someone who appears to have more or be better. A more helpful approach is to compare yourself to who you were yesterday. God didn't create you to be that other person or to have their gifts and abilities. In His infinite wisdom, God created you to be uniquely you.

Name 3 amazing gifts or abilities God has blessed you with:

1.

2.

3.

"If you want to experience the flow of love as never before, the next time you are in a competitive situation, pray that the others around you will be more outstanding, more praised, and more used of God than yourself. Really pull for them and rejoice for their success. If Christians were universally to do this for each other, the earth would soon be filled with the knowledge of God's glory." — Dallas Willard in The Spirit of Disciplines

Take Action

This week, when you feel envy beginning to creep up, try following these 3 steps:

- Become aware of your envious thoughts. Can you change them right away by removing yourself from the situation or counting the many blessings God has gifted you? Simply becoming aware of the thoughts and taking control of your mind is the first step.

- Pray that God will meet you where you are and help you overcome your negative thoughts and feelings. Surrender your mind to Him. Focus on Him and His many blessings, as we are reminded in Colossians 3:1-2: "Since, then, you have been raised with Christ, set your hearts on things above, where Christ is, seated at the right hand of God. Set your minds on things above, not on earthly things."

- Pray for the person that is causing you to envy. Pray that the gifts, talents, and abilities God has given that person can be fulfilled to God's glory. Learn to offer simple prayers of blessing over even the people you envy, and your capacity to love may grow all the more.

Day 2 – Search Me God

Today's Bible Verse

Read: Psalm 139:13-24

Reflection

Reread verses 17-18. What is the significance of these verses? Whether God's thoughts are directed to us or are about us, one thing is clear: we are immensely valued by God, and we are always on His mind. His thoughts toward us are so vast that they cannot be counted; they outnumber the grains of sand. How does this verse make you feel about yourself and your value to God?

"Search me, O God, and know my heart; test me and know my anxious thoughts. See if there is any offensive way in me." In this prayer, David was inspired to worship and praise God. Yet, in the midst of his prayer, he begins to picture those who are rebellious toward God. He pauses in his worship and cries out, "Do I not hate those who hate you, O Lord...? I have nothing but hatred for them." But as he considers others who may live lives not fully submitted to God, he begins to wonder if there might be a place in his own heart that isn't fully surrendered. With great courage, he asks God to search his heart, to test him, and to reveal anything in him that isn't fully submitted to God.

Have you ever prayed that prayer? Are you willing to pray that prayer? It might feel risky to ask God to search you, but it's a prayer we must all pray if we are truly serious about growing. When we pray that prayer, the Holy Spirit will answer. Take a moment now to speak to God.

Take Action

- Read Psalm 139:13-24 once more, being open to praying a "search me" prayer.
- Notice where the Holy Spirit's spotlight is shining. Is there something in your life that pulls you down spiritually, something the Holy Spirit is urging you to release? Perhaps it's a relationship that needs refining, struggles with anger, or an inability to let go of grudges. Maybe it's time to repent, trust, and leave something behind—time to let it go.

Day 3 - Spiritual Gifts

Today's Bible Verse

Read: 1 Corinthians 12:12-26

Reflection

We each have God-given abilities, or spiritual gifts. Our spiritual gifts are specifically chosen for each of us by God—for our good and for the good of others. It's our responsibility to discover our spiritual gifts and then develop and exercise them with the help of the Holy Spirit. While no Christian possesses every gift of the Spirit, every Christian has some of God's wonderful gifts. To effectively grow as Christians, we must find and use these gifts.

"There are different kinds of gifts, but the same Spirit distributes them. There are different kinds of service, but the same Lord." —1 Corinthians 12:4
Here are some of the spiritual gifts you may have been given by God:

Administration - The ability to organize multiple tasks and groups of people to accomplish these tasks

Apostleship - The strength or ability to pioneer new churches and ministries through planting, overseeing, and training

Craftsmanship - The ability to plan, build, and work with your hands in construction/building environments, specifically to accomplish multiple ministry applications

Evangelism - The ability to help non-Christians take the necessary steps to come to know and have a relationship with Christ

Exhortation - The gift of being able to strengthen, comfort, or urge others to action based on Biblical truth

Faith - The strength or ability to believe in God and His unseen workings in every area of life

Giving - The ability to produce wealth and to give for the purpose of advancing the Kingdom of God on earth

Healing - The strength or ability to heal physical, mental, and spiritual sickness

Hospitality - The ability to create warm, welcoming environments for others in places such as your home, office, or church

Intercession - The ability to stand in the gap in prayer for someone, believing for profound results

Leadership - The ability to influence, direct, and focus people to a big picture, vision, or idea

Mercy - The ability to feel empathy and to care for those who are hurting in any way

Pastor/Shepherd - The ability to care for the personal needs of others by nurturing and mending life issues

Service - The ability to do small or great tasks in working for the overall good of others

Teaching - The ability to study and learn from the Scriptures, specifically with the purpose of bringing understanding and depth to others

Word of Wisdom - The ability to understand and bring clarity to situations and circumstances, often through applying the truths of Scripture in a practical way

After looking them over, take note of the ones you feel you have been gifted with. Then, throughout the course of the week, look for these gifts in others. Notice how recognizing the gifts others have been given makes you feel. Does it spark any envy or any feelings of self-doubt or insecurity not having the same gifts?

Try to recognize the gifts you've been given and the gifts of those around you, and then take the mindset that each different gift has been given for the glory of God and the unity of the body of Christ.

Additional Reflection

- We all face the temptation to envy others. While being tempted isn't a sin, allowing envy to take root and fester can be destructive. Envy divides people and destroys relationships, and it can manifest in nearly any situation: at work, at school, in our marriages and families, and even in our service to God.
- "For where envy and self-seeking exist, confusion and every evil thing are there." —James 3:16
- Can you think of instances where envy has caused a division between you and someone you know? What actions or feelings stemmed from your envy? How did it weaken the unity God desires for you to build with others?

"John 17:11-13 - I will remain in the world no longer, but they are still in the world, and I am coming to you. Holy Father, protect them by the power of your name, the name you gave me, so that they may be one as we are one. I in them and you in me—so that they may be brought to complete unity. Then the world will know that you sent me and have loved them even as you have loved me."

Take Action

Comparing ourselves to others and feeling envious not only wastes our time but also squanders the opportunities we have to grow into the people God created us to be. It robs us of joy.

Envy does not promote God's best for our lives; it hinders our growth in faith, love, gratitude, and happiness.

Imagine if, instead of envy, we focused on cultivating virtues!

Yes, we all have limitations and weaknesses, and there will always be others who are "better" or more gifted in certain areas. But rather than dwelling on that, we can choose to focus on the spiritual gifts we've been given and the works God has prepared for us.

When we do this, we come to see that we fit into the Body of Christ exactly as we should, flourishing as the unique individuals God created us to be.
This allows us to become useful members of the Body of Christ, working together with others in unity and harmony.

Day 4 – Light in the Darkness

Today's Bible Verse

Read: Ephesians 5:1-17

Reflection

In today's reading, Paul writes to the church in Ephesus, urging them to be a witness in the world using a powerful image: the world is in darkness, and Christians are the light that illuminates it. When followers of Jesus live in a way that pleases the Lord, with actions that are "good, right, and true," people will see Christ in them. Paul encourages the Ephesians to be a light in the world, echoing what Jesus says about Himself in the Gospel of John (John 8:12). Paul reminds us that as we wait for the coming of Christ, we are called to be His light in the world, reflecting His presence.

How can you be a light in the world? To whom might God be calling you to reflect His light? What is God asking of you?

Consistently being Christ's light in the world isn't easy. In what areas of your life do you struggle most with reflecting His light to others? Are there times when that light has dimmed in your life due to worry, stress, or a sense that God is distant? Ask God to be present with you in your worries and stress. Pray for the grace to see Him more clearly each day and to bear more fruit in the areas where you struggle.

Take Action

- Read Ephesians 5:1-17 once more. As you conclude your time in scripture and prayer today, pray for forgiveness for the times you have neglected to be in light to others, and commit yourself more deeply to shining the light of Jesus to others.

Day 5 - Forgiveness & Mercy

Today's Bible Verse

Read: John 8:1-11

Reflection

Jesus doesn't condemn the woman caught in adultery ("Neither do I condemn you"), but neither does He condone her actions ("Go and leave your life of sin"). This distinction separates guilt from shame. Guilt is the recognition that we've done something wrong; shame is the belief that "I am wrong."

How might Jesus' approach help you confront and deal with your own sin? What changes might He be calling you to make? In what situations might He be saying to you, "I don't condemn you, but go and do _____ no more"?

Take a moment to speak to Him about this now. Honestly acknowledge the areas where you may be falling short—those areas of sin in your life. Bring these situations before God without shame, and ask for His strength to go and sin no more.

We can easily fall into the trap of having a judgmental, condemning attitude toward others, perhaps even wanting to "throw a stone" at them. It's important to be self-aware of what "pushes your buttons." What are some of your triggers—situations or people—that draw out an angry, defensive, or judgmental attitude in you? In which situations do you struggle to respond with mercy and grace? What helps you to respond well in challenging moments?

Take Action

- Choose one or two very specific areas in your life that you feel most tempted to sin - any area, situation, or relationship in which you believe you fall short of God's best version of you. Where might God be calling you to grow?
- Focus on that this week, and hear Jesus' words spoken to you: "I love you. I accept you. But I want you to go and do this no more."
- Likewise, take note of any "triggers" that might make you prone to judgmental, angry, or condemning thoughts. Be aware of these triggers, and when they arise, pause and ask Jesus to help you find a heart that is less condemning and more loving; a heart filled with grace.

Day 6 – The Rule of Life

Today's Bible Verse

Read: Colossians 3:17 & 1 Corinthians 10:31

Reflection

These verses offer us a "rule of life," a plan of action that helps us align our daily activities with the ultimate goal of pursuing God's kingdom. Whatever we do, we are called to do it all in the name of the Lord. Is pursuing God's kingdom truly the goal of your life? How committed are you to pursuing this goal?

Think specifically about three daily activities where you can apply this rule of life. How can you put this principle into action in those activities? How can you approach them in the name of the Lord? Make a conscious effort to focus on Jesus' presence with you, especially during these moments.

Take Action

- Read Colossians 3:17 & 1 Corinthians 10:31 once more. As you read and reflect, ask God for His help and guidance to be more like Him if He were in your place.

Week 4 Devotionals

Transform Daily

Day 1 – The Lord's Prayer

Today's Bible Verse

Read: Matthew 6:5-13

Reflection

Today's passage contains what is commonly known as "The Lord's Prayer," although it might more accurately be called "The Disciples' Prayer," as it serves as a model for those who follow Jesus. This model of prayer is set within Jesus' teaching against hypocritical religious practices. Jesus was contrasting the self-serving actions of many religious leaders with the way true followers of God should behave. These leaders were motivated by a desire to draw attention to themselves rather than to simply exalt and honor God. After describing the wrong way to pray, Jesus offered a new model, beginning with the words, "Our Father in Heaven…" Why do you think He chose to start this way? (See Rom. 8:14-16; Eph. 2:18-22; Matt. 7:7-10)

Jesus addressing God as "Father" was unexpected in the Jewish culture of His day. Judaism had many reverent names for God but did not commonly refer to Him as "Father." This would have been surprising, perhaps even controversial, to His listeners. Jesus clearly wanted to emphasize God's closeness and personal availability to His followers in prayer.

This opening is immediately followed by the phrase, "Hallowed be your name." Consider what it means to "hallow" God's name. The word "holy" means to be "set apart" or "different." Notice that Jesus begins by addressing God as Father and then quickly calls us to focus on God's holiness. Why do you think He structures the prayer this way?

Do you tend to view God more as a tender Father or as a perfect and powerful God? While He is both, we often lean toward one perspective over the other in our prayers. How might your prayers change if you focused more on God as a tender and loving Father, but minimized His perfection and power? Or if you saw Him as perfect and powerful, but less as a tender and loving Father? Spend a few moments reflecting on how you most often view God and how this perspective might influence your prayers.

Take Action

- "Your kingdom come, your will be done, on earth as it is in heaven." When we pray for God's kingdom to come, we're not just anticipating a future event. While we look forward to the day when Jesus will return and establish His kingdom in its fullness, this prayer also asks for God's plan to be carried out now, here on earth. Every time you sincerely seek to obey God and carry out His will—whenever you strive to live and love like Jesus—you are bringing His kingdom into the world through your actions.
- How is He calling you to bring His kingdom into the world today? How can you bring a glimpse of His kingdom to those around you?

Our mission should be to make the world more like His kingdom, even if our reach only extends to our family, neighborhood, and community. God desires you to bring His kingdom to those around you, making this world reflect more of His heavenly kingdom.

Day 2 – Self Care

Today's Bible Verse

Read: Mark 1:35-37 & Mark 6:30-32

Reflection

How did Jesus model self-care in these verses? Despite His short time on earth, why do you think He often took time away from ministering to others to retreat and recharge?
When you fail to properly care for yourself, what is usually the cause? What are the typical results when you neglect self-care? Be specific.

In Deuteronomy 5:12-15, God commands the Israelites to observe the Sabbath. What do you think is the connection between His reminder of His great power in verse 15 and their need to rest on the Sabbath? How can trusting in God's power and goodness help you take time each week for a Sabbath rest from your activities?

Take Action

- Read Mark 1:35-37 & Mark 6:30-32 once more. Imagine Jesus' words in Mark 6:31 being spoken directly to you.

Day 3 - Daily Bread

Today's Bible Verse

Read: Exodus 16:1-21

Reflection

The Israelites were provided with daily bread in the form of manna. What connections do you see between the Israelites' experience and Jesus instructing us to pray for our daily bread? What do you think God was trying to teach the Israelites by requiring them to depend on daily manna? How might you apply that lesson to your life today?

"And lead us not into temptation, but deliver us from the evil one."
Why do you think Jesus specifically references "the evil one" in His model for prayer? What reality about the spiritual world do you think He wants us to be aware of? With God's strength, we are empowered to stand against temptation and the evil one.

"No temptation has overtaken you that is not common to man. God is faithful, and He will not let you be tempted beyond your ability, but with the temptation, He will also provide the way of escape, that you may be able to endure it." —1 Corinthians 10:13 (ESV)

"Submit yourselves therefore to God. Resist the devil, and he will flee from you." —James 4:7 (ESV)

What temptations are you currently facing that you may need to bring to God for strength? Perhaps the temptation is to withhold love from someone, to fail in honoring God or others in your words or actions, or to not reflect God's love in a way that brings Him glory. Maybe you're tempted toward actions or words that you know don't reflect God's best for your life.

Take some time to reflect. What temptations in your life are pulling you away from becoming the person God created you to be?

Take Action

- Read through Matthew 6:9-13 once more in its entirety. Read it slowly, phrase by phrase, reflecting on its meaning and considering how the truth of the passage relates to you in your life right now. Choose one phrase to take with you throughout the course of the week. Consider how God may want this phrase to strengthen you, or how He may be calling you to change and grow.

Day 4 - Does God Know Best?

Today's Bible Verse

Read: 1 Kings 17:7-16

Reflection

In today's reading, both Elijah and the widow demonstrate remarkable faith and courage. Trusting God can be challenging because we often want to control and fix our situations ourselves. However, there is a direct correlation between the daily hope you experience and your ability to walk by faith each day. How confident are you that God knows what is best for you, even when you can't see a solution? How capable are you of placing your problems in God's hands and letting His peace fill your heart?

God's instructions to Elijah, and Elijah's directions to the widow, may have seemed illogical—likely the last thing either of them would have chosen to do. But Jesus says in Luke 11:28, "Blessed rather are those who hear the word of God and obey it." Is there something in your life that you feel God might be asking you to do, something you may not want to do?

Take a moment to reflect honestly on this. Then, tell God that even though you may not want to, or even if you don't fully understand, you will choose to trust and obey Him.

Take Action

- Read 1 Kings 17:7-16 once more. As you move through the next week or so, choose to start each day by telling God you plan to trust and obey Him. Throughout your day, trust Him and obey Him even when you don't want to. And then end each day by thanking God for the hope He has given you.

Day 5 – Stop Your Worry; Stop Your Hurry

Today's Bible Verse

Read: Matthew 6:24-34

Reflection

Why do you think Jesus tells His listeners not to worry in these verses? How does worry keep you from truly seeking the kingdom of God and from experiencing all the treasures God has in store for those who seek Him?

When worry or anxiety begins to intrude upon your peace, try taking a few moments of solitude. Jesus often practiced silence and solitude—intentional time spent alone and quiet with God and with our own souls. This practice creates space for God to speak to us. Consider two dimensions of silence and solitude: external and internal. Externally, find a place away from people and noise, put your phone aside, and seek out a spot where you won't be disturbed. Internally, calm and slow your mind, and rest in God's presence. You might choose to sit still and listen for what God might want to say to you, dive into Scripture, or spend time in prayer. Start with just 5-10 minutes as you build the habit of sitting before God and casting your anxieties on Him.

What do you think is the difference between being busy and being hurried? What personally makes you feel hurried?

Dallas Willard once called hurry "the great enemy of spiritual life in our day." Much of our anxiety and worry stems from a constant state of hurry. We often live with a sense of fatigue, anxiety, and a relentless feeling of being rushed. We move through our days at breakneck speed and then wonder where God is in the midst of it all.

The truth is, many of us are too busy to live our most emotionally healthy and spiritually vibrant lives.

Take Action

- Consider the following statement: "Hurry is evidence of a disordered heart, not a disordered schedule." How have you seen hurry affect your spiritual life, such as your ability to spend time with God, to love others, or to be fully present with people?
- Your challenge this week is to work to eliminate hurry from your life. This doesn't mean you need to stop being busy. It means you need to train yourself away from the kind of hurry that keeps you constantly worried, anxious, or preoccupied. It means you need to work to slow down enough to fully love and receive love, to spend time with God, and to be present in each and every moment with others. It's a big challenge! Be aware this week when hurry, anxiety, worry, or feelings of being overly preoccupied begin to creep up. Take a deep breath, slow down, and ask God to give you a heart characterized by peace and love.

Day 6 - God's Healing

Today's Bible Verse

Read: John 4:43-54

Reflection

We often think of healing in terms of miraculous cures—a crippled man casting aside crutches or someone in a wheelchair suddenly able to walk. But healing can also happen in small, everyday ways. It can occur through the quiet goodness of God's grace or the unexplainable peace that comes with His presence. How have you experienced healing? Has God's grace helped you heal from past hurts, disappointments, guilt, or anger?

Sometimes we're blind to God's healing presence. As you reflect on situations where you've experienced healing, can you recognize how He might have used another person to bring healing into your life? Or how He may have used you to bring healing to someone else?

Is there anyone in your life who may need God's healing—whether physical, emotional, or spiritual? Where do you see God in this situation? Can you take a moment to pray for that person now?

4o

Take Action

- Read John 4:43-54 once more. As you read it, focus on the fact that this same Jesus who brought miraculous healing in this story is the same Jesus you are spending time with now.

Week 5
Devotionals

Transform Daily

Day 1 – Sit Before Jesus

Today's Bible Verse

Read: Luke 10:38-42

Reflection

Why was Mary commended, and what was Martha missing? Who do you relate to more in this story—Mary or Martha? In what areas of your life do you sometimes find yourself acting like Martha?

If you tend to be more like Martha—always busy and rarely sitting still to fully embrace the presence of Christ—consider this question: What work might God long to do in your life that He can only accomplish if you become more intentional about sitting quietly at His feet?

Read: John 12:1-8

In John 12:4-5, Judas is also angry with Mary. How does his anger differ from Martha's in the earlier story?
Didn't Judas have a point? Wasn't this an extravagant waste? Compare and contrast Jesus' response to Martha in Luke 10:41 with His response to Judas in John 12:7.

What was it about Mary that so impressed Jesus? Reflect on both passages you've read. Do you sometimes get so busy with good, even "Christian," activities—perhaps even church-related—that you neglect to spend time simply sitting before, adoring, and listening to Jesus?

Take Action

- In the week ahead, make a deliberate choice to spend time alone with Jesus. Intentionally put Him first—allow Him to lead you in every situation you face. Choose to follow Jesus and let Him guide your steps.
- Remind yourself continually: I cannot go faster than the One who is leading. Repeat this phrase throughout the day. Write it down on a sticky note and place it on your mirror or desk. If you truly desire for God to be in control of your life and to follow Christ as His disciple, you need to slow down and follow the pace of the One you've chosen to lead you.
- Resolve to take each day one activity at a time. If you start becoming preoccupied with the next thing, stop. Entrust the moment to God and return to the needs of the moment.

Day 2 – Tested By God

Today's Bible Verse

Read: Genesis 22:1-12

Reflection

Abraham was a man of great faith, but even his faith was tested. As he remained faithful and endured, his faith was strengthened, refined, and perfected. Look back at the passage. How did Abraham respond to God's request (v. 1-3)? How long did it take to reach the place God had directed him to go (v. 4)? Imagine what this journey must have been like for Abraham—the dark and lonely moments he must have faced as he grappled with the seeming contradiction of God's promise.

When the moment finally came, Abraham was willing to do what God had called him to do (v. 10-12). What would need to happen in your heart, in your relationship with God, for you to reach such a place of obedience and trust? God calls us to keep walking in faith, even when things seem impossible. Reread Genesis 22:1-12, and ask God to help you become so transformed that you can continue walking in faith, no matter what difficult situations you may be facing.

Take Action

- Reread Genesis 22:1-12 and ask God to help you become a transformed person who can continue walking in faith regardless of the difficult situations you may be facing.

Day 3 - Abide in Christ

Today's Bible Verse

Read: John 15:1-10

Reflection

Jesus says that if we remain in Him, we will bear much fruit. What fruit do you believe He wants you to bear in your life right now?

Just as a branch is nurtured and fed by the vine, we are called to abide in God to properly nourish our spiritual growth. What does it mean for you to abide in God? What actions do you take to feel most connected to Him? Do you connect through prayer, fellowship, or time spent reading the Bible? Reflecting on the past week, how easy was it for you to connect with and abide in Christ? What obstacles did you face in trying to do so?

How can you abide in Christ in your moment-by-moment living? Not just during quiet times or moments set aside for prayer or Scripture, but throughout your entire day—how can you intentionally abide in Christ?
"And whatever you do, whether in word or deed, do it all in the name of the Lord Jesus, giving thanks to God the Father through him." —Colossians 3:17

Take Action

- In the week ahead, be attentive to the opportunities God may provide for you to abide in Him. This might include spending a little extra time in the Bible each morning or offering continuous prayers throughout your day for strength and peace.
- Consider each challenging or difficult situation you encounter as a means by which God is training and strengthening you in your spiritual journey. Whenever you face a difficult, annoying, or trying situation, ask yourself: How can this moment be a training ground for me? How might this moment teach me patience and graciousness? How might it help me develop self-control?
- This week, look for opportunities for growth. Be willing to see every trial, no matter how big or small, as a chance to become more of the person God has created you to be.

Day 4 – Make Jesus Central

Today's Bible Verse

Read: Luke 19:1-10

Reflection

Zacchaeus was a despised man. In that time, tax collectors were deeply hated in the Jewish community because:

- They were notorious for being thieves, gaining wealth by extorting money from taxpayers.
- They were seen as traitors to their own culture. Roman governors appointed Jewish men as tax collectors for Jewish regions, so they were despised for betraying their own people to ally with the pagan Roman government.

Based on what you know of this story, what do you think Zacchaeus thought about himself before encountering Jesus?

Zacchaeus' focus on money shifted dramatically (v. 8) when he met Jesus. Jesus became the new center of his life. Why do you think Zacchaeus—a wealthy man by all indications—would choose to give up so much after meeting Jesus?

Jesus must also be central in our lives. When He is, everything else falls into its proper place. When Jesus became central in Zacchaeus' life, his approach to people and money transformed, now reflecting his new relationship with Jesus. As Christians, we are called to align every area of our lives with our relationship with Jesus. What areas of your life do you struggle most with aligning your actions, thoughts, and attitudes around your relationship with Him? In what ways is it freeing to approach life with Jesus at the center of your actions, words, and attitudes?

Read Luke 19:1-10 once more, reminding yourself that, just like Zacchaeus, you are loved and accepted by Christ.

Take Action

- Reflect on the areas of your life that need realignment with Jesus at the center. Throughout the week, make a conscious effort to place Jesus at the heart of your decisions, actions, and thoughts. Pray for the guidance and strength to keep Him central in every aspect of your life.

Day 5: Faith & Actions

Today's Bible Verse

Read: James 2:14-28

Reflection

Consider how your faith is demonstrated through your actions. Where might God be calling you to serve, love, forgive, or encourage others? To what extent do people see your faith reflected in your actions? Do your actions truly align with your faith? What actions, words, or attitudes might God be convicting you to change?

1 John 3:16-18 says, "This is how we know what love is: Jesus Christ laid down His life for us. And we ought to lay down our lives for our brothers. If anyone has material possessions and sees a brother in need but has no pity on him, how can the love of God be in him? Dear children, let us not love with words or speech but with actions and in truth."

Reflect on examples from your own life that might mirror the situation described in James 2:15-16: "Suppose a brother or sister is without clothes and daily food. If one of you says to them, 'Go in peace; keep warm and well fed,' but does nothing about their physical needs, what good is it?"

Take Action

- Perhaps you know someone who needs help with childcare or a ride to the airport. Maybe there's a family going through a tough time that could use a homemade dinner, a lonely neighbor who would appreciate a visit, or an aging parent in need of care. This love can also be shown through simple acts of service for your family—making dinner, doing laundry, helping with homework, or extending patience and forgiveness. Any action done to serve others in love reflects God's heart. What opportunities has God placed in your life to love others in action and truth?

- As you begin each day in the week ahead, pray that God will open your eyes to every opportunity to love and serve those around you. Encourage someone who needs it, demonstrate kindness and patience, lend a helping hand, or offer a favor without expecting anything in return. You may be surprised by how your own joy flourishes as you move through your day seeking ways to be a blessing to others.

56

Day 6 - What's Competing with Jesus?

Today's Bible Verse

Read: Mark 12:28-34

Reflection

To love God with all your heart, soul, mind, and strength, He must be at the center of your life. What things in your life are competing with Jesus for that central place? This might become apparent by what consumes most of your attention or focus, what drives your actions and words, and how you spend your time. What are the signs that something other than Jesus has become central to your life and decision-making?

Proverbs 3:5-6 says, "Trust in the Lord with all your heart, and do not rely on your own understanding; in all your ways acknowledge Him, and He will make your paths straight." What does it mean to acknowledge Him in all your ways?

Take Action

Take a few moments and consider what it looks like to make Jesus central in the following areas of your life. Don't hold back. Reflect, and honestly answer the questions for each area.

- Relationships:
- Finances:
- Time/Schedule:

  o What are you doing to make Jesus more central to this area of your life?
  o In what ways are you failing to make Jesus more central to this area of your life?

Read Mark 12:28-34 once more, taking time to ask God to make clear to you all the ways you can better love Him with all your heart, soul, mind, and strength.

Week 6
Devotionals

Transform Daily

Day 1 – Joy & Peace

Today's Bible Verse

Galatians 5:22-25

Reflection

Would you consider yourself a joyful person? Do you find that you become easily irritable? How often do you laugh and have fun? It's easy to feel happy when circumstances are good, but do you maintain joy regardless of your current circumstances, trials, or troubles? Are you able to remain joyful even during times of frustration or difficulty?

In 2 Corinthians 6:10, Paul says that Christians can be "sorrowful, yet always rejoicing" (ESV). This means that even in situations that bring genuine sorrow, our inner joy remains intact. At the core of our being, we can rejoice in the fact that we are loved children of God. Our joy is strengthened when we remember that, no matter what the circumstances, God is with us, God loves us, and God is in control.

Would you describe yourself as a peaceful person? To what extent do you bring peace and harmony to stressful situations? Would others say they feel more peaceful and relaxed in your presence?

"You will keep in perfect peace him whose mind is steadfast, because he trusts in you." (Isaiah 26:3)

We are not promised a life without troubles, but we are promised something better—God's peace in the midst of trouble. God keeps in perfect peace those who (1) "whose mind is steadfast" and (2) "who trusts in you." Both expressions require faith: the first engages our mind, the second our heart. What is the difference? With our mind, we believe; with our heart, we trust. With our mind, we believe in the goodness and sovereignty of God, and with our heart, we trust Him to fulfill His promises.

Take Action

The key to cultivating the fruit of the Spirit isn't a secret; it's simply something we often overlook. Seek God, and His Spirit will produce its fruit in you.

- In the week ahead, reflect on the ways God brings life, joy, and peace to you—whether through nature, art, serving, worship, spiritual friendships, scripture, exercise, family, rest, long conversations, or solitude.

- How can you intentionally incorporate these life-giving activities into your schedule?

- Seek God's joy. Seek God's peace. As you begin to flourish in these areas, let it overflow to bless those around you. Be so joyful that others feel encouraged and uplifted in your presence. Be so filled with peace that those around you find comfort and ease. Flourish, so that your life becomes a blessing to those around you.

Day 2 – What Are the Results of Your Sin?

Today's Bible Verse

Read Genesis 3:6-10 & Psalm 32:1-4

Reflection

Genesis 3:6-10

Why did Adam say he was hiding? Do you think there was more to his response? Why do you think he was avoiding God? What emotion was he feeling?

Psalm 32:1-4

What were the results of David's hiding? What do these verses reveal about human tendencies in prayer when sin is present?

It is crucial that we learn to pray even in the midst of our sin. We can be certain that we will continue to struggle with sin on this side of eternity. Perhaps you're battling internally with anger, pride, envy, greed, or a self-seeking heart. Reflect on the areas of sin you struggle with most. We all wrestle with sin, but rather than isolating these struggles from our prayers, we need to bring them before God. Talk to Him about what's happening inside that you know displeases Him. Place your disobedience in the arms of the Father; His arms are strong enough to carry the weight. As Emily Griffin writes, "The Lord loves us most of all when we fail and try again."

Take Action

- Read Genesis 3:6-10 and Psalm 32:1-4 again.
- Consider how your prayer life might change if you truly laid everything before God—your hopes, struggles, and fears.
- Reflect on the areas of sin you struggle with the most. How can you bring these struggles to God in prayer?
- Pray for the strength to be honest with God about your sins and to seek His guidance and forgiveness.

Day 3 - Patience, Kindness, & Goodness

Today's Bible Verse

Read: 1 Corinthians 13:1-10

Reflection

You've likely heard the cliché, "Patience is a virtue." Paul lists patience as one of the fruits of the Spirit in Galatians 5:22-23, so there's no doubt that, as Christians, we are called to be patient. Patience can be defined as waiting without complaint. At first glance, it may not seem like a particularly significant moral trait—what's so virtuous about not complaining?

Under ordinary circumstances, patience might not be difficult to practice. However, in the face of trials, discomfort, or simply annoying situations, patience becomes much more challenging. What are the situations where you find it hardest to remain patient? "Be completely humble and gentle; be patient, bearing with one another in love" (Ephesians 4:2). And with which people do you struggle the most to be patient and bear with in love? Bring these situations and people to God now. Ask that the love and peace of Christ dwell in you so fully that you find the strength needed to be patient in these circumstances and with these individuals.

Kindness and goodness are closely related, so much so that it's sometimes difficult to distinguish between them. We often think of a kind person as a good person, and a good person as naturally kind. Both traits stem from love. The kindness mentioned in Galatians 5:22 comes from the Greek word *chrestos*, which refers to a gracious disposition in character and attitude. It is tender, compassionate, and sweet.

The word *chrestos* is also used in Luke 5:39 to describe fine, aged wine that is mellow or sweet, without bitterness. This helps us better understand what Paul is saying in Ephesians 4:31-32 and 5:1-2:

"Get rid of all bitterness, rage, and anger, brawling and slander, along with every form of malice. Be kind and compassionate to one another, forgiving each other, just as in Christ God forgave you. Be imitators of God, therefore, as dearly loved children, and live a life of love, just as Christ loved us and gave himself up for us as a fragrant offering and sacrifice to God."

When compared to *chrestotes*, goodness is the practice or expression of kindness—it's the act of doing good. Goodness, therefore, involves serving and ministering to one another. It is a spirit of generosity put into action through service and giving. Goodness naturally flows from kindness. All of this is encapsulated in the word love, for love is kind and good, always seeking to meet the needs of others.

Reflect on God's kindness and goodness toward you. Consider His deep, tender compassion for you and recall the many ways He has expressed this kindness in your life. For "every good and perfect gift is from above," given to you by a God who loves you more than you can comprehend. In what ways has God shown His kindness and goodness to you?

Take Action

God has shown you tremendous kindness and goodness, and He calls us to extend that same kindness and goodness to others.

"Give, and it will be given to you. A good measure, pressed down, shaken together, and running over, will be poured into your lap. For with the measure you use, it will be measured to you." (Luke 6:38)

- In the week ahead, seek out opportunities to lend a helping hand, even when you're busy, or to assist someone without expecting anything in return.
- Take time to encourage and affirm others.
- Go out of your way to say something kind, or offer assistance, help, or support to someone who hasn't asked for it.
- Be purposeful and intentional in showing the kindness and goodness of God to those around you.

Day 4 – Where Are You God?

Today's Bible Verse

Read: Psalm 13

Reflection

Some prayers in the Bible are known as "Prayers of Complaint" or "Lament Prayers," many of which were written by David, "a man after God's own heart." Psalm 13 is an example of such a Lament Prayer. Does it feel uncomfortable to address God in this way? Why or why not?

How does David's understanding of God prevent these prayers from turning into chronic complaining? How can you remain rooted in humility while praying with such honesty?

Think about a time in your life when you felt forgotten by God. Perhaps you've experienced—or are currently experiencing—a period of waiting, struggling with thoughts of sorrow, or feeling like your prayers are unanswered. Reflect on that time or bring your current situation to mind.

Now reread this part of the verse: "But I trust in your unfailing love; my heart rejoices in your salvation. I will sing the Lord's praise, for he has been good to me." How has God been good to you, even during difficult times? Even when you didn't feel His presence? How has He shown His goodness and grace in your life? Be specific, and think of a few examples now.

Take Action

• Read Psalm 13 once again, noticing which portions of this Psalm stand out to you today. Consider writing your own Lament Prayer to God, expressing your honest emotions and then reaffirming your trust in His goodness.

Day 5 – Do People See Jesus in You?

Today's Bible Verse

Read: Colossians 3:1-17

Reflection

When people see you, do they see Jesus? How so? What characteristics of Christ do you demonstrate to others? What Christ-like traits might God be calling you to exhibit more often?

When people are with you, do they experience greater joy and peace, or do they feel conflict and stress? With whom do you find it easiest to bring a sense of joy and peace? And with whom is this the most challenging?

"Therefore, as God's chosen people, holy and dearly loved, clothe yourselves with compassion, kindness, humility, gentleness, and patience" (Colossians 3:12).

When you struggle to reflect Christ to others, remind yourself: "I am chosen, I am holy, I am loved." As someone who is chosen, holy, and loved, you are equipped to love others with the love of Christ.

"So, if you think you are standing firm, be careful that you don't fall! No temptation has overtaken you except what is common to mankind. And God is faithful; he will not let you be tempted beyond what you can bear. But when you are tempted, he will also provide a way out so that you can endure it" (1 Corinthians 10:12-13).

The key to fighting temptation and pursuing self-discipline is the deep belief that the pleasures of a future reward are worth the denial of current, lesser pleasures. It's this belief that nourishes the spiritual fruit of self-discipline—desiring the rewards the Spirit offers more than the fleeting rewards that sin or the world provide.

What are your greatest sources of temptation? In what areas of your life do you struggle most to wholeheartedly follow Jesus and live in a way that reflects Him to others?

Take Action

When athletes lose motivation, their coaches and trainers encourage them to keep their eyes on the prize. This is the same encouragement we receive in 1 Corinthians 9:24-27:

"Do you not know that in a race all the runners run, but only one gets the prize? Run in such a way as to get the prize. Everyone who competes in the games goes into strict training. They do it to get a crown that will not last, but we do it to get a crown that will last forever. Therefore I do not run like someone running aimlessly; I do not fight like a boxer beating the air. No, I strike a blow to my body and make it my slave so that after I have preached to others, I myself will not be disqualified for the prize."

Remember: sustained self-discipline is fueled by a deep desire for more joy in God, both now and in the life to come. Focus on the eternal rewards, and let them motivate you to reflect Christ in all you do.

Day 6 – Go Into All the World

Today's Bible Verse

Read: Mark 16:15-20

Reflection

In today's reading, just before returning to the Father, Jesus sends out His followers to spread the good news. How do these verses resonate with you? Do they make you feel enthusiastic, cautious, encouraged, or perhaps inspired to dedicate your life more fully to God?

The signs of being a follower of Christ likely aren't about handling deadly snakes or drinking poison unharmed. So, what are the true signs that indicate you are a follower of Christ? What might others see in you that marks you as a disciple? How can you demonstrate in your daily life that you have chosen to follow Jesus?

Even after Jesus returned to the Father, we are told that "the Lord worked through them." In what ways have you experienced the Spirit of Jesus working in and through you?

Take Action

- Read Mark 16:15-20 once more.
- Notice exactly what it is that Jesus tells the disciples to do, and how they respond.
- Ask God for the gifts that you need to proclaim the good news through your life.
- Reflect on specific ways you can show others that you are a follower of Christ and ask for the strength and courage to live out your faith boldly.

Week 7
Devotionals

Transform Daily

Day 1 – Dealing with Anxiety

Today's Bible Verse

Read: Philippians 4:4-9

Reflection

Anxiety isn't fun.

Chances are, you or someone you know struggles with anxiety. It's that overwhelming feeling of being consumed by "what ifs." What if this goes wrong? What if this happens—or doesn't happen? Anxiety is a state of trepidation and apprehension.

While anxiety and fear are related, they are not the same. Fear is a response to something actually going wrong, triggering the fight-or-flight reaction. Anxiety, on the other hand, is the worry that something might go wrong.

Many factors can contribute to anxiety. Here are a few:

Change: Not just change itself, but often the accompanying feeling of losing control. Anxiety often arises when life suddenly feels out of our control, increasing as our sense of control diminishes. Those who desire control over everything tend to be the most stressed.

Feeling hurried, rushed, and over-busy: We move faster than ever before, juggling schedules that seem nearly impossible to manage. This constant rush leaves us struggling to be present, always thinking about what needs to be done next or what was left undone. Keeping up with our own lives can lead to anxiety.

Personal challenges: These might include financial troubles, job loss, health battles, relationship struggles, addictions, divorce, or the loss of a loved one. Life's challenges can leave us feeling depleted and anxious.

Day 1 – Dealing with Anxiety

Today's Bible Verse

Read: Philippians 4:4-9

Take a few moments to reflect. What is currently causing you the greatest anxiety? Bring these concerns before God now.

Read Isaiah 41:10:

"So do not fear, for I am with you;
do not be dismayed, for I am your God.
I will strengthen you and help you;
I will uphold you with my righteous right hand."

Now, personalize this verse by turning it into an "I" statement:

I will not fear, for You are with me.
I will not be dismayed, for You are my God.
You will strengthen me and help me;
You will uphold me with Your righteous right hand.

Take Action

- In the week ahead, keep Paul's words, "Do not be anxious about anything," at the forefront of your mind. This phrase is written in the present active tense, implying an ongoing state. In other words, don't allow your anxiety to become a constant presence.
- While feelings of anxiety are unavoidable, remaining trapped in them is optional.
- When you feel anxiety beginning to rise, pause, take a deep breath, acknowledge what's causing your anxiety, and bring it before God in prayer. Don't allow yourself to live in the prison of perpetual anxiety.

Day 2 – Are You Walking Through the Desert?

Today's Bible Verse

Read: Exodus 13:17-22

Reflection

When Pharaoh let the people go, God didn't lead them on the most straightforward path. After leaving Egypt, they only needed to cross the Sinai Peninsula—a journey of less than 200 miles that could have taken just a few weeks. But God had an alternate route in mind, thinking, "If they face war, they might change their minds and return to Egypt." So He led them along the desert road toward the Red Sea—a hot, dry, barren wasteland, far from the shortcut they would have preferred. You can almost hear the grumbling starting and the fear rising. And this was just the beginning of their journey.

What "desert" experiences have you encountered? Everyone goes through a time in the desert—a period when faith feels hard, God seems distant, or you struggle to understand why God is allowing such a dry, barren, and difficult experience.

God had promised His people that He would lead them to a land full of blessing. This destination was worth fighting for and worth going the distance. But the journey there would stretch their faith, leading them through trials where they'd have to depend on God like never before. We face similar journeys as God leads us toward our own "promised land." Maybe you feel like the blessing is too long in coming, or perhaps you're tempted to give up. Be assured today that God is faithful, and He will use all things to strengthen our faith and bring goodness to His people. Stay strong, keep pressing on.

On these desert journeys, there may be questions that go unanswered or confusion that remains unresolved. Still, we must choose: Is there hope on the other side of the desert? Can even a barren place lead to life? Will this stretch of time, with all its ups and downs, trials, and tests, eventually lead home? Are you in the desert right now? If not, you may be soon.

Remember, God has not abandoned you. He has not forgotten you. It may not seem like the quickest or easiest path, but God has a plan. He is far less concerned with how you get there or how long it takes than He is with *who you will be when you arrive.*

Take Action

- Read Exodus 13:17-22 once more. God led His people then with a pillar of cloud and a pillar of fire; how might

- He be guiding you right now?

- Reflect on how God is guiding you through your current circumstances.

- Take time to pray and ask for His guidance, strength, and reassurance as you navigate your own desert experiences.

Day 3 – Let Go of the Need to Be in Control

Today's Bible Verse

Read: John 6:1-13

Reflection

There are times when our anxiety stems from our desire to be in control. We want to manage the circumstances around us and guarantee the outcomes in our lives. However, this often backfires, and as our sense of control diminishes, our anxieties increase. But rather than trying to control everything, God calls us to trust in Him. He wants us to trust in His goodness and His plan, even when we don't understand what He's doing. He wants us to rely on His strength and His sovereignty.

What areas of your life does this resonate with? Where might you benefit from letting go of control and allowing God to be in charge?

Isaiah 43:2 says:

"When you pass through the waters, I will be with you; and when you pass through the rivers, they will not sweep over you. When you walk through the fire, you will not be burned; the flames will not set you ablaze."

Think about the situations that bring you worry. Consider the areas in your life that feel overwhelming or nerve-racking. What causes you concern? Bring these situations to mind, and now picture God walking with you through each one. Know that He is with you. Become aware of His presence and experience a sense of release as you trust more fully in His control.

Take Action

- Reflect on the areas in your life where you feel the need to be in control.

- Bring these areas to God in prayer, asking Him to help you trust in His control and plan.

- When you feel anxiety rising, remind yourself of Isaiah 43:2 and visualize God walking with you through each situation.

- Practice releasing control to God and trusting in His strength and goodness.

Day 4 - Christ Has Chosen You

Today's Bible Verse

Read: John 15:18-27

Reflection

"I have chosen you out of the world." Jesus has called you to follow Him and to be a light in the lives of others. As a disciple of Jesus, you are invited to participate in His mission to redeem the world. If you have experienced Christ as your salvation, He wants you to help others experience Him as well.

How would you describe your goals as a disciple of Jesus? What do you think His goals are for you as His disciple?

How do you believe He wants to use you in your life? Who in your life do you think He wants you to bless? How might He want you to be a light to others?

There will be times when people respond to you as a follower of Jesus with joy, feeling blessed by your words and actions as you share the gospel. But there will also be times when people respond negatively. As a disciple of Jesus, you may experience persecution in various forms. You might feel confused, frustrated, or even angry at times.

When have you encountered negative interactions or emotions in your efforts to follow Jesus?

On the other hand, what rewards have you experienced as a disciple of Christ? How have you seen Him work through you in the lives of others?

Take Action

Read John 15:18-27 again, keeping in mind that just as Jesus encountered trouble while working to redeem the world, we will too. By modeling His courage, love, and unwavering focus on His purpose, we can persevere and grow into fruitful disciples of Christ.

- Reflect on how Jesus has called you out of the world and what that means for your daily life.

- Consider specific actions you can take to be a light to others and to bless those around you.
- Pray for the strength and courage to respond to any negative reactions or persecution with love and grace.

- Focus on the rewards and positive impacts of following Jesus, and thank Him for the opportunities to serve Him.

Day 5 – There is Power in Prayer

Today's Bible Verse

Read: Genesis 24:1-15

Reflection

"Before he had finished praying, Rebekah came out with her jar on her shoulder."

There is power in prayer. God invites us to bring our concerns to Him, to express what's on our minds, what we're worried about, and what we're dealing with. These prayers can emerge throughout the day, in the midst of our activities, and during difficult or trying situations. How often do you pray during the day? When faced with a problem or a challenging situation, how likely are you to pause and pray in that moment?

1 John 5:14 says, "This is the confidence we have in approaching God: that if we ask anything according to his will, he hears us."

How confident are you that God hears your prayers?
Would you pray more if you had greater confidence and faith that God is listening?

Take Action

In the week ahead, become mindful of the moments when you start to feel anxious, preoccupied, worried, or overwhelmed.

Whether it's a problem, a person, or a particular situation causing these feelings, be proactive in your response. Pause and lift the situation—and your anxiety—up to God. Remember, as 1 Peter 5:7 says: "Cast all your anxiety on Him because He cares for you."

Know that God is there, eager to hear from you and to replace your worry with His joy.

"Rejoice in the Lord always. I will say it again: Rejoice!"

We are told—commanded even—to rejoice! God wants us to be joyful. Jesus told His friends that His desire for them was to be filled with joy, but not just any kind of joy: "I have said these things to you so that my joy may be in you, and that your joy may be complete."

How joyful would you say you are these days?

Do you think others would see you as a joyful, peaceful person, or as someone more rushed and anxious?

When you find yourself leaning toward anxiety rather than joy, bring one of these verses to mind:

- "Delight yourself in the Lord, and he will give you the desires of your heart." —Psalm 37:4

- "May the God of hope fill you with all joy and peace in believing, so that by the power of the Holy Spirit you may abound in hope." —Romans 15:13

- "Go, eat your food with gladness, and drink your wine with a joyful heart, for God has already approved what you do." —Ecclesiastes 9:7

- "Let the sea roar, and all that fills it; let the field exult, and everything in it! Then shall the trees of the forest sing for joy before the Lord, for he comes to judge the earth. Oh give thanks to the Lord, for he is good; for his steadfast love endures forever!" —1 Chronicles 16:32-34

- "Therefore I tell you, do not be anxious about your life, what you will eat or what you will drink, nor about your body, what you will put on. Is not life more than food, and the body more than clothing? Look at the birds of the air: they neither sow nor reap nor gather into barns, and yet your heavenly Father feeds them. Are you not of more value than they? And which of you by being anxious can add a single hour to his span of life?" —Matthew 6:25-27

Day 6 – The Mindset of Christ

Today's Bible Verse

Read: Philippians 2:5-11

Reflection

These verses are often referred to as the "Hymn to Christ." This passage beautifully captures both Jesus' identity and His mission in the world. What is your initial reaction to verse 5? Does this seem possible to you?

What do these verses reveal about Jesus' mission in our world?
We often think of the incarnation as being driven primarily by our desperate need for salvation—that Jesus came into the world because humanity needed Him so urgently. While it's true that we are all sinners and utterly hopeless without Christ, it's essential to understand that God, not us, was the primary motivation for the incarnation. In verses 6-7, Paul emphasizes that Jesus is God, existing "in the form of God" from the beginning. Yet, He humbled Himself and became obedient to death—not to us, but to God. He was never obligated to us; His obedience was entirely to the Father.

What difference does it make to view Jesus' mission as one of obedience and service to God, rather than merely coming to serve our needs?
Jesus Himself confirmed His motivations when He said to the crowds, "For I have come down from heaven, not to do my will, but the will of Him who sent me" (John 6:38).
On a practical level, what does it mean to serve and obey God? What does that look like in your life? How can you align your actions with God's will, just as Jesus did?

Take Action

- Read Philippians 2:5-11 once more, open to what God may want to say to you in these verses.

- Reflect on how you can adopt the mindset of Christ in your daily life.

- Consider specific actions you can take to serve and obey God more fully. Pray for the strength and humility to follow Christ's example of obedience and service.

Week 8
Devotionals

Transform Daily

Day 1: Are You Content No Matter the Circumstances?

Today's Bible Verse

Read: Philippians 4:10-20

Reflection

"I have learned to be content whatever the circumstances."

That's quite a statement! How content do you feel, regardless of your circumstances? What are the things in your life that leave you feeling discontent? When do certain moments, situations, people, or thoughts steal your joy, contentment, and peace? And what do you think the "secret" is, as Paul puts it, to being content in any and every situation?

We can't be content when we allow our minds to be filled with negative thoughts. Romans 8:31 tells us, "If God is for us, who can be against us?" If God is for you, shouldn't you be for yourself? The words you speak to yourself have power, and if you repeat them often enough, they become your "truth." When you dwell on negative thoughts about yourself, you rob yourself of the joy and contentment God desires for you.

Paul wrote:

"No, in all these things we are more than conquerors through Him who loved us. For I am convinced that neither death nor life, neither angels nor demons, neither the present nor the future, nor any powers, neither height nor depth, nor anything else in all creation, will be able to separate us from the love of God that is in Christ Jesus our Lord."

Now, personalize this passage with your own sources of anxiety:

"No, in all these things I am more than a conqueror through Him who loved me. For I am convinced that neither bills nor debt, neither work demands nor poor body image, neither problems with my in-laws nor tomorrow's to-do list, nor any bad news, neither insecurities nor failures, nor anything else in my busy life, will be able to separate me from the love of God that is in Christ Jesus my Lord."

Take Action

This week, try to take note of every time you feel anxious. What thoughts are causing your anxiety? For example:

- "I'm worried about my kids."
- "I'm fighting with my spouse again. This is too much."
- "The bills are out of control this month; how are we going to pay them?"
- "I've gained so much weight. If I can't love myself, who could possibly love me?"
- "My job feels unstable. What if I lose it?"

Pay attention to the situations or events that trigger your anxiety. How did they make you feel, and how did you react? Then, try to identify the core fear behind your anxieties. Is there a common theme? How many of the things you worried about actually materialized or became real problems? Notice how many of your worries never amounted to anything—other than worry. Finally, observe how your worries and anxieties affected your relationships with those around you. Simply becoming aware of our anxieties, what causes them, and the impact they have on us is a significant step in managing them.

Read Philippians 4:10-20 again, focusing especially on verse 19. Savor each word, memorize it, and keep it at the forefront of your mind.

Day 2 – Hard Pressed Yet Hopeful

Today's Bible Verse

Read: 2 Corinthians 4:7-12

Reflection

Paul paints a grim picture of his life in these verses—feeling hard-pressed, persecuted, and struck down. Yet, there is a thread of hope woven throughout.

- How would you express that hopeful note in your own words?
- To what extent do you feel that same hope in your life?
- What do you think you need in order to maintain a similar positive and hopeful perspective on your own experiences?
- Why do you think Paul was able to remain positive even in the midst of pain?
- What personal barriers, such as hurry, anxiety, fatigue, anger, or selfish ambition, keep you from being as positive as you could be?

Take Action

Read 2 Corinthians 4:7-12 again, but in this reading, continue all the way through verse 18.

- Take encouragement from Paul's positive and hopeful attitude, even in the face of challenges. Reflect on how you can cultivate a similar outlook in your own life.
- Consider practical steps you can take to overcome personal barriers and focus on the hope and positivity that your faith provides.

Day 3 – Get Out of Your Boat

Today's Bible Verse

Read: Matthew 14:22-33

Reflection

From Peter's perspective, what happened after Jesus revealed His identity to the disciples? What was significant about Peter's response, and how did it impact the disciples (see v. 33)?

Fear of failure often prevents us from "stepping out of the boat." Some might view Peter's walk on water as a failure, but is the bigger failure not having attempted it at all, as the others did by remaining in the boat?
Jesus invited Peter to step out of the boat and walk to Him—asking Peter to do something impossible on his own, something that required God's power and presence.

In what areas of your life might God be calling you to "get out of the boat"?

How might He be asking you to demonstrate faith greater than fear and to trust Him wholeheartedly?

Take Action

As you think about "getting out of your boat" to follow Jesus fearlessly, live your life fully for Him, and love others deeply, consider the following questions:

- Looking back at your life, when have you taken risks and accepted challenges? When have you allowed fear to keep you from stepping out of the boat? How have these decisions—whether bold or cautious—affected your life?
- Would you describe your relationship with God right now as dynamic and growing, or stagnant and stale? Are there ways He may be calling you to make a change in your relationship with Him?
- Are you more of a risk-taker or a comfort-seeker? Could you be avoiding what God is calling you to do because it feels risky? Ask God to give you the courage to seek Him fully and live for Him to the absolute fullest.

Return to Matthew 14 and read verses 31-33 once again, imagining yourself as Peter in that scene.

Day 4 – Run the Race

Today's Bible Verse

Read: Hebrews 12:1-3

Reflection

Today's verse speaks of running the race with perseverance. What do you need to lay aside in order to do so? What might that look like for you personally?

What does it mean to fix your eyes on Jesus? On a practical level, how can you incorporate this into your daily life?

How can the following verses from the book of Hebrews help you find comfort in fixing your eyes on Jesus during difficult times?

- Hebrews 2:17-18
- Hebrews 4:15-16
- Hebrews 5:8-9
- Hebrews 7:23-25

Take Action

- Read Hebrews 12:1-3 once more, feeling encouraged to put aside anything that may be holding you back from running the race God has set before you to the best of your ability.
- Reflect on specific actions you can take to "lay aside" obstacles and focus on Jesus in your daily life.

Day 5 – Armor of God

Today's Bible Verse

Read: Ephesians 6:10-20

Reflection

Today's reading presents a powerful metaphor for the action we need to take in our spiritual lives. Paul sets the scene for us as one of warfare, but our battle isn't against people or worldly enemies; it's against the evil one. Take a moment to consider what keeps you from consistently putting on the full armor of God.

What prevents you from staying keenly aware of the spiritual battle raging around you? Most likely, it's the cares and distractions of daily life that cause you to neglect putting on God's armor.

Reflect on each piece of armor and consider when you're least likely to put it on:

- **The belt of truth:** For you, this might mean resting, trusting, and finding peace in the truths God reveals about Himself in His Word. When do you struggle most to keep the belt of truth securely fastened around your waist?

- **The breastplate of righteousness:** If we don't protect ourselves with righteousness, we leave ourselves vulnerable to the enemy's attacks. To be righteous means obeying God's commands and living in a way that honors Him, even in the small, seemingly insignificant moments. When is this the most challenging for you?

- **Your feet fitted with the gospel of peace:** Do you bring peace with you wherever you go? Is peace evident in your actions?

- **The shield of faith:** This should protect your mindset, your heart, and give you a sense of security. Does it? When does it not?

Taking time to evaluate these areas can help you stay equipped and ready for the spiritual battles you face each day.

- **The helmet of salvation:** This is your ultimate protection. This is a vital piece of equipment as without it, a warrior could experience instant death. How much thought and attention do you give this crucial piece of armor on a day-to-day basis? You are loved. You are saved.

- **The sword of the Spirit:** This is the word of God. The better you know the word of God, the more capable you will be to use it. You can't just pick up a sword and expect to know how to use it effectively, efficiently, and successfully. You must train with it. You must spend time learning how to use it. You must prepare. How prepared do you feel to use the word of God as a sword?

Take Action

To be strong in the Lord, Paul encourages us to "pray in the Spirit on all occasions with all kinds of prayers and requests." Whether you're doing housework, spending time with family, waiting in a long line at the grocery store, dealing with someone who requires patience, or even exercising, lift your prayers up to God. Simple prayers like "Thank you, God," "Help me, God," "Give me patience, God," or "Please give me the strength I need" can make all the difference.

Consider the prayer requests found in the following verses. Are these ever requests you bring to God?

- Mark 9:24
- Luke 17:5
- James 1:5
- Psalm 38:22
- Matthew 5:44
-

Today's passage concludes with a final prayer request for strength. Notice Paul's desire: "whenever I speak, words may be given me so that I will fearlessly make known the mystery of the gospel."

You may not have an evangelical mission trip planned or be preparing to go abroad to share the good news of the gospel with those who have never heard it. You may not experience even a fraction of what Paul faced as an "ambassador" for Christ. But you have the opportunity to reflect Christ to the family God has placed you in. You have the chance to let others see Christ through you in your community, workplace, and neighborhood.

Whenever you speak, you have the opportunity to live as Christ would if He were in your shoes. The words you choose, the tone you use, and even your body language all have the potential to bring the gospel into someone else's life simply by reflecting Jesus.

Can you pray for the strength to do this now?

Ask God that in every situation—whether trivial or difficult, insignificant or challenging—you may be given the words and the ability to live as an ambassador of Christ.

Day 6 – Put This Above All Else

Today's Bible Verse

Read: 1 Corinthians 13:1-3

Reflection

What are the actions or achievements Paul mentions in this passage that, when done without love, amount to nothing?

Is Paul overstating his point or exaggerating? Why or why not?

Imagine Paul is writing directly to you. Rewrite verses 1-3, replacing the actions and achievements with those you are often tempted to elevate above love.

Now, read 1 Corinthians 13:4-7. Paul uses 15 words to describe love. After reading this passage, summarize the qualities of love in your own words.
Look at 1 Corinthians 13:4-7 again, and notice that you can replace the word "love" (or the pronoun "it") with "Jesus." The passage still makes perfect sense.

Now, try replacing the word "love" with your own name. In what ways do you embody these aspects of love? In what areas do you need to grow to better demonstrate these qualities?

Take Action

To conclude, read John 15:1-10. What is the one thing ultimately required of you if you are serious about continuing to grow as a disciple of Christ?

You've completed the final devotional in this Transform Daily 8-week challenge!

It's been an honor to spend these past 8 weeks with you, and I hope that in some way, you've been blessed, strengthened, or inspired.
God bless you as you continue in your faith journey!
Till next time!
Kelly :)

95

ABOUT THE AUTHOR

Kelly Wenner is the founder and creator of SoulStrength Fit, SoulStrength Fit Kids, and SoulStrength Fit Devotionals, as well as the podcast Devotionals on the Go, which offers quick, daily reflections.

Her passion is to help busy Christians live strong, vibrant lives, growing in their walk with the Lord.

Kelly is dedicated to empowering others to feel their best physically and spiritually. Her mission is to help people deepen their faith, strengthen their relationship with God, and honor Him by honoring their bodies. She strives to inspire others to live out their greatest potential and become the best version of themselves that God has created them to be.

Kelly lives in Southern California with her husband and three daughters.